For Dorothy –
fellow author
& great companion,
Mary Wade

Aug 13, 1987

Milk, Meat Biscuits, and the Terraqueous Machine

The Story of Gail Borden

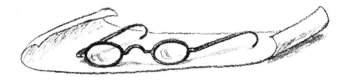

Mary Dodson Wade

EAKIN PRESS ★ Austin, Texas

Illustrations and cover art by Nancy Grobe.

For Amy
    whose book it should have been

Contents

About
Gail Borden

Everyone knows about Borden's milk and ice cream, but Gail Borden, the founder of the company, was many more things than just a dairyman. He played an active role in early Texas history. His creative mind dreamed up many inventions, most of them not very successful. He was universally admired for his honesty.

Gail came to Texas in 1829 and became a trusted friend of Stephen F. Austin. He surveyed, kept land records, and collected taxes. He made the first topographic map of Texas. He published the first permanent newspaper in Texas. His company printed the Texas Declaration of Independence as well as William B. Travis's letter from the Alamo. He was the first customs collector for the port of Galveston. He was also a partner in the Galveston City

Company, which controlled the city for seventy-five years.

A man who couldn't sleep, he kept busy with his inventions — some of which were practical, some not. The meat biscuit could have served a purpose, but it was not appetizing. It was his memory of crying children that spurred him to make condensed milk.

Most of his business deals were done simply with a handshake. Stephen F. Austin, shortly before his death, wrote to James Perry, "Who can I trust? Gail Borden. He is conscientiously an honest man."

Gail Borden did not let what others said about him keep him from doing what he thought was right. Many Galveston citizens thought he was strange or at least a meddler because of his ideas. He wrote what could have been his epitaph: "I am rewarded in the consciousness of having done some good."

Most of the conversation in this book has been created to give a sense of the time and the people, but all the events are true.

2

In a Hurry

The tall schoolteacher came running down the road.

"Here comes Mr. Borden!" yelled Pollard.

"I'm ready!" answered Charlie.

The boys stood beside the road to the Bates Schoolhouse in Amite County, Mississippi. The sun was not up yet on the warm spring morning in 1824.

Gail Borden didn't even stop as he reached down for Charlie. He swung the little boy up to his shoulders. Pollard ran beside them. He had to take two steps for each of the teacher's long ones, but he didn't mind. Tomorrow it would be his turn to ride on Mr. Borden's shoulders.

When they got to the clearing, Charlie slid down.

"Why do you always run?" asked Pollard, puffing from running so hard.

Gail Borden bounded up the stairs and unlocked the door. "I have to ring the bell at sunrise," he said.

Charlie looked up at his teacher. "My daddy says you run so your feet can keep up with your mind."

The boys trailed behind their teacher as he went inside. "You talk funny," said Pollard.

Gail Borden's dark eyes twinkled. "Oh, I'm a Yankee all right," he said. "Or at least I started out that way."

In one step he was over at the map. "I was born here in Norwich, New York. Then, when I was thirteen years old, we moved a thousand miles west," he said, tracing the route with a long finger. "I helped my father survey the town of Covington, Kentucky. Two years after that we went west again to Indiana."

"Wow!" said Charlie, "I've never lived anywhere but here."

Gail Borden nodded as he moved quickly to the door. "My bad cough is much better here in the south."

The boys kept up their questions as they followed the teacher to the door. "Were you really in the army?" asked Pollard.

"Something like an army," said the teacher. "The farmers formed a militia."

"And you were the general," said Charlie.

"I was a captain," answered the teacher. "Line up, students. It's time for school."

4

The $200
Bride

Two years later, Gail Borden paced nervously in the office of the marriage clerk. He was twenty-six years old.

"Sign here, Captain Borden," said the clerk.

Gail read the piece of paper then turned to the sixteen-year-old young woman beside him. "Well, Miss Penelope, do you think you are worth $200?"

"Why, Mr. Borden, how you talk!" said Penelope.

Gail teased her. "This paper says that we can't get married unless I have $200."

Penelope Mercer couldn't believe it. "Do you really have to pay that much?"

"Oh, not exactly," laughed Gail. "I just have to prove that I have enough money to provide for a

5

family. Now that I am land surveyor I guess I can afford a wife. Give me that pen!"

He took the pen and signed in large letters GAIL BORDEN, JR.

At the wedding, everyone crowded around. "Congratulations, Borden. That's a fine wife you're getting," said the men.

Gail Borden beamed down at his new bride. The Baptist minister's daughter smiled up at her tall husband.

Gone to Texas

One day a letter came. "It's from your brother," said Penelope.

Gail read the letter.

> San Felipe de Austin
> State of Coahuila and Texas
> Mexico
> April 3, 1829

My dear Gail,
 I am writing this letter to beg you to come to Texas. All the family is here now except you.
 Texas is a wonderful place. The Mexican government gives settlers 4,000 acres. The land is good for raising crops. Cattle graze year 'round. There is great opportunity.

> Your brother,   Thomas Borden

Texas was not a state yet. It was a colony of Mexico, and Americans were going there to settle on the land.

Penelope knew her husband well. "We can go," she said. "My mother and father are going."

Gail Borden's eyes danced. "That's it!" he said, "We'll do it!"

Then his face sobered. "Are you sure you can make the trip?"

"I will go wherever you go," said Penelope.

Soon they were on a boat for New Orleans.

At New Orleans Gail and Penelope took a steamer. Gail paced the deck during the whole trip. As Galveston Island came into view, Gail shouted, "There it is!" But Penelope was too tired to care.

Their ship docked along Buffalo Bayou on December 24, 1829, just in time for their daughter Mary to be born.

Texas Land Surveyor

The capital of the colony, the little town of San Felipe de Austin, sat perched on a high bank of the Brazos River. It was a scattering of log houses on the long road between San Antonio and the Louisiana border.

"Welcome to Texas," said Stephen Austin, shaking Gail's hand. They stood in the office of the man who had brought American settlers to Texas. "Your brother Tom has been very busy," said Austin. "I'm sure he will be glad to have your help with the surveying."

Gail went to work right away measuring and marking the land for new settlers. For his own family he chose a place twenty miles down the river, near Fort Bend. He built a house and began to raise cattle.

During the next several years Gail not only traveled the countryside but also raised cattle on his farm. Two sons were born.

One Sunday the Bordens were keeping a quiet Sabbath. Gail walked along with Penelope at his side. He had Henry Lee perched on his shoulder. Penelope carried baby Morton Quinn. They paused at a small grave. Penelope placed a handful of flowers on it. "Little Mary," she said softly, "we miss you."

Gail had more and more surveying work to do because his brother Tom kept going off somewhere else to look at land.

Penelope got impatient. "It's not right for you to be gone so much," she said.

Gail continued to gather his things. "Someone has to check the boundaries and settle disputes."

Penelope folded her arms. "Just tell them to settle things themselves."

"But, Penelope, this job helps me to know the country," he said as he filled his saddle bags. "Did I tell you that a New Orleans company has asked me to make a map of Texas?" he said excitedly. "And I'm going to do it! This will be the best map Texas ever had because I know this land!"

Newspaperman

Texas was a good place to live, but Stephen Austin was worried. "We are Mexican citizens, but we are too far from the government. The officials in Mexico City don't know what we need."

The settlers wanted changes. "Texas should be a separate Mexican state," said some of them. "Maybe then the government would care about us."

"Perhaps a committee could straighten things out," said Austin. "Borden, I want you to serve on it."

"I'll do it," said Gail.

Fifty men came to San Felipe to try to solve the problems. At one of the meetings Sam Houston was present. "Borden," said Houston, "help us write a constitution for Texas as a separate state."

Gail and the others set to work immediately. When the paper was finished, Stephen Austin

We will keep the people informed.

picked it up. "I will take it to Mexico City myself," he said.

"That's a thousand miles from here," protested Houston.

"I must do this for my people," replied Austin.

Gail stood up and reached his long arm across the table to shake hands. "We will take care of things while you are gone," he said.

"I trust you, Borden," said Austin.

Months went by. The Bordens moved to San Felipe. Gail worked day and night. He did many things Austin would have done. He made sure people got the right land. He wrote letters to people who wanted to come to Texas.

One day Gail came home with bad news. "The Mexicans have put Austin in jail."

"But he was trying to work things out," said Penelope.

"We need a newspaper," said Gail. "That will let everyone know what is going on."

"You have never worked on a newspaper, but you were a teacher," said Penelope. "I think you would make a good newspaperman."

"I'll do it!" said Gail, pacing around the room, gesturing with his long arms. "We'll call it the *Telegraph and Texas Register* because this newspaper will give out news, and it will faithfully record events."

Gail, and his brother Tom, and Joseph Baker formed Baker and Bordens Printing Company. The other two then went away, leaving Gail to do most of the work.

The first issue of the paper appeared on October 10, 1835. Penelope looked at it. "Texas isn't even mentioned till the third page!" she said.

"We want to give our readers information on many things," answered her husband, his pen scratching away on an article for the next issue. When one hand got tired, he switched to the other one. The writing looked the same.

The week the first issue came out, people at San Felipe were all talking about a mysterious bright light in the sky every night. The newspaper explained, "This is the comet predicted by Dr. Edmund Halley to make its appearance this year."

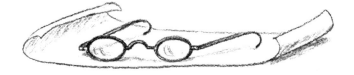

War!

Many months went by. Stephen Austin was still in jail in Mexico City. At San Felipe the settlers were angry with the way the Mexican government was treating them and their leader.

Finally, Austin returned to Texas, but he knew the idea of peace was hopeless. "The dictator Santa Anna will not listen to us," he said.

"We don't need Mexico!" shouted one man.

"Right!" said another. "Texas isn't going to be a Mexican state. We're going to be a free nation!"

Gail attended meetings. There was talk of war and invading Mexican armies. Gail was appointed to the Committee of Safety for the town.

With all his other duties, he never stopped the paper. "We will keep the people informed," he said.

One day the dreaded word came. The Mexican army was marching into Texas. That night Gail

Borden printed a bulletin with a big headline: "WAR."

He worked day and night now. There was little time for sleep. Getting out the paper was hard work. Joseph Baker went off to join the army. Paper was hard to get. People didn't pay for their copies.

Penelope worried about her husband. He was trying to publish the paper, collect the taxes, and keep the land office. "It is all right, Penelope," said Gail. "I will do the best for my country, praise or no praise."

The new Texas government needed time to get organized. They moved to Washington-on-the-Brazos to get farther away from General Santa Anna and the Mexican army, but Gail kept his printing press in San Felipe. The Texas government made Baker and Bordens their official printer. Riders carried documents back and forth between the two towns.

On March 2, 1836, the delegates fifty miles away made a great decision and then quickly sent back the news. The light burned late in the offices of the *Telegraph and Texas Register* as they printed a very important document.

"Here it is," Gail said, showing it to Penelope. "The Texas Declaration of Independence!"

The next issue of the paper carried the headline: "Texas Has Declared Its Independence." The paper also printed an apology to two signers of the Declaration of Independence. In the rush to print the document that night, their names had been left off.

The Runaway Scrape

It was a dark night several days later when a lone rider came into San Felipe. Soon the whole town heard crying.

"That's Miss Cummings," said Penelope. "I must go see about her."

Soon she ran back to the print shop. "The Alamo has fallen. Miss Cummings was engaged to marry William Travis. Now he and all the brave men who defended the Alamo are dead!"

Gail kept lights burning late again at the newspaper office, printing the terrible news.

People panicked. Mexican General Santa Anna was coming with a huge, well-trained army. Sam Houston had only a handful of farmers, and he kept retreating.

Settlers, fearing for their lives, fled eastward to safety in the United States. They left everything behind — cattle, crops, and belongings.

"Penelope, take the children and go to Father's house," said Gail. "And take these land records with you. They must be kept safe also."

"Come with us," said Penelope.

"No," answered Gail. "I will stay here to print the news. As long as there is a newspaper west of the Brazos, everyone will know Texas is all right."

The Mexican army got closer and closer. There was no way to save San Felipe. To keep Santa Anna from using the houses, everything was burned to the ground.

Gail spoke to his brother, "Let's get the press over the river. We'll take it to Harrisburg, where the government is now."

They dragged the heavy printing press to the river bank. Once they got on the other side, the press sank down in the mud. There were no oxen or carts to carry the press. Finally, they got it on a boat and headed for Harrisburg.

Santa Anna's army marched eastward, getting closer to Harrisburg each day. Sam Houston retreated again. The Texas officials fled from Harrisburg just hours before the Mexicans arrived.

But Gail Borden's press did not escape. The printers were still working to get out an issue when the Mexicans seized the press.

The *Telegraph and Texas Register* did not get to print the glorious news of Sam Houston's victory over the Mexicans at San Jacinto. During the eighteen-minute battle that made Texas free, the press lay at the bottom of Buffalo Bayou, where Santa Anna had ordered it to be dumped.

Galveston Storm

The war was over. Texas was a free country, but the Bordens had lost almost everything. Their house and barns had been burned. Gail was wearing the only clothes he had.

The government of the Republic of Texas did not have enough money to pay for Gail's printing press. He could not even get them to pay for the Texas Declaration of Independence he had printed.

The Bordens lived for several months in Columbia, which was supposed to be the new capital, but Gail finally sold his part of the newspaper and moved his family to Galveston.

President Sam Houston did not forget the way Gail had helped during the revolution. He knew Gail Borden was an honest man, so he picked him for a very important job.

Gail came bounding home. "I'm the new customs collector," he told Penelope. "Many ships come to Galveston carrying all kinds of goods. The ship owners have to pay a tax on everything that is for sale. I will collect the tax on those things."

One day Gail came home very mad. "Imagine!" he said to Penelope. "That man stood right there and told me that those boxes were all for himself! He had twelve trunks of clothes, eighteen boxes of furniture, a box of sausages, five boxes of preserves, and an organ."

"That does seem a lot," said Penelope.

"A lot!" shouted Gail, throwing up his hands. "It's a whole store! If he thinks he is going to sell everything and not pay taxes, he'll find out what kind of collector I am!"

Gail was at his desk in one step. "And if that's not enough, smugglers were on the other side of Point Bolivar today." He grabbed a pen and paper. "I'm writing to President Houston right now. They have got to give me a patrol boat so I can control the bay around Galveston Island."

Gail worked long and hard at his job. Penelope was proud of him. "But that old customs house where you work is a disgrace. Why, you just have a box for a desk, and you have to sit on a barrel," she said.

When a new customs house was built, Gail proudly accepted the keys. Two days later, he walked up to the second story to look out at the ships in the harbor. Suddenly, a storm came up. "Better get home," he said, closing the doors and windows.

The wind blew. The rain beat down. Hour after hour, waves crashed on the island.

When the hurricane passed, Gail hurried off to see about the city. He walked up and down the streets. Houses and buildings were knocked down. Lumber had been thrown everywhere.

Then, he heard the fire alarm ringing. "I was afraid this would happen," he said.

When he got to the fire, he stormed over to the man who had carelessly started it. "Sir," said Gail, shaking his finger in the man's face, "If this happens again, you will be arrested!"

Penelope met him at the door when he came back. "How is the new customs house?" she asked.

"It's gone," said Gail. "Even the papers in that iron trunk from New Orleans are ruined."

"How dreadful," said Penelope. "I guess the old customs house is gone, too."

"That's the funny part," said Gail. "There were eighty soldiers in it. They weighed so much the building could not float away. I'll move my office to a ship in the harbor until another customs house can be built. We'll put the next one higher above the water."

Doing Well

Another year went by. Sam Houston was no longer president of the Republic of Texas.

Gail paced back and forth. He nearly stepped on four-year-old Morton Quinn, who was playing on the floor. Six-year-old Henry Lee scooted out of the way. "Mirabeau Lamar will never make a good president," said Gail. "Now he has fired me as customs collector."

"I liked it when you were at the customs house, Papa," said Henry Lee. "I liked it when Sam Houston came. I liked the big guns they shot off, and the Indian chief who came."

Penelope picked up Philadelphia who was toddling around.

"Papa, Papa," said the little girl, holding out her arms to her father.

"Your little daughter likes you," said Penelope

with a laugh. Then her face got sober. "You are a good man, Gail Borden," she said.

"Not everybody thinks so," answered Gail. "There were plenty of people who didn't like it when I told them to clean up after the storm because it was a fire hazard. They said I was acting like a sheriff, that I didn't have any right to do that."

Gail stopped pacing for a moment. "But I am rewarded to think that I have done some good."

Galveston Landowner

A year later, the family stood beside the bed where Penelope lay with a tiny baby in her arms. "What is his name?" asked Morton Quinn.

Gail peered down and said, "We'll call this third boy Stephen F. Austin Borden," said the proud father.

Penelope smiled. "That's a good name," she said.

The children played with the baby's tiny fingers, but Gail began to pace around the room. "What is bothering you now?" asked Penelope.

"Water!" said Gail. "The whole bay is full of water, but still Galveston does not have enough. All our drinking water has to be brought in by boat."

"What can you do?" asked Penelope.

Gail jammed his hat on. "I'm going to find some!" he said.

For days he tramped along the beaches. He had people digging everywhere.

One day he came running home. "We found it, Penelope. We found it!"

Not long after that there was a knock at the door. Penelope wiped the flour from her hands as she answered it. Three faces peered out behind her. In the other room baby Stephen was crying.

The man bowed. In a French-Canadian accent he said, "Good morning, Madame. I am Michel Menard. Is Mr. Borden home?"

"Come in, please," said Penelope. "Children, go find your father."

Henry Lee found his father hunched over some drawings.

"What's that?" asked Henry Lee.

"It's a machine I thought of," answered his father.

"Oh," said Henry Lee. "Mama says there is a man here who wants to talk to you."

Gail Borden went to the parlor. He shook hands with the man.

"Mr. Borden," said Michel Menard, "the people on the island are grateful that you found water for us."

"It is no more than any citizen would have thought it his duty to do," answered Gail.

"But you are the one who did it," answered Mr. Menard. "We are going to have a great city here.

25

We'll advertise and sell lots. We need your help in surveying."

Penelope beamed. "Mr. Borden and his brother laid out the city of Houston. They were very clever to put the streets southwest to northeast so that the gulf breeze would make things cooler."

Michel Menard nodded. "We know of this," he said. "Now, Mr. Borden, for your help, you would have part interest in our company and get your choice of lots."

Gail thought a minute then held out his hand. "I'll do it," he said.

Long after the man left, Gail sat looking over the map. Penelope found him there at midnight. "You old stay-awake," she said. "What are you planning now?"

"We're going to build our house right here," said Gail, pointing to a corner lot. "This is where 35th Street and Avenue P cross."

"Those are not very interesting names," said Penelope.

"But they make sense," said Gail. "You can't get mixed up where everything is."

Every day the workmen came. The house began to take shape. Henry Lee and Morton Quinn raced up and down the unfinished stairs. "We'll be able to see the world from up here!" Henry Lee told his brother.

"I see ships," said Morton Quinn.

Penelope carried baby Stephen Austin and Gail

held the squirming Philadelphia. "This observatory really is nice," said Penelope.

"Just think," said Gail. "When we came to Galveston, there were just two families living here. Now there are nearly 2,000 people from every nation and more coming every day."

Henry Lee tugged at his father's coat. "Papa, the ships have flags. Where is our flag?"

"A flag," said his father. "Of course, a flag!"

He set Philadelphia on the floor and ran downstairs to the workmen. "We must have a flagpole!" he called.

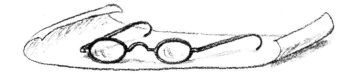

Craziest Man in Town

Two boys peeped through the high fence around the house on 35th Street. "What's he doing now?" asked one.

"He's working on a big wagon," said the other.

"Let me see," said the first one. He peeked through the hole. "He's putting a sail on the wagon!" said the boy.

"On the wagon?" asked the other, trying to push his way to the hole.

"Yeah," said the first one. "Now he's pulling the wagon out of the shed. It looks like a boat rolling on the land."

Suddenly, Gail Borden came around the corner of his fence. The boys ran away, talking about the strange machine.

Later that evening, a crowd of people followed

"Sit still!" yelled Gail. *But no one paid any attention.*

29

Gail Borden to the beach. The ladies were laughing, and the men were having a good time, too.

At the beach they stared at his latest invention. "Mr. Borden, what do you call this thing we're going to ride in?" asked one lady.

"It's my terraqueous machine," he replied.

"What an amusing name," said another woman.

"It is a good Latin name," replied Gail. "*Terra* means land and *aqua* means water. This machine will go on land and water."

"Let's get going then," cried one man.

They all piled into the wagon. The wind caught the sails. The wagon rolled along the beach faster and faster.

"Sit down!" said Gail.

The wind pushed the wagon even faster. It rolled into the water. Just then a big wave caught the wagon. It began to rock. The ladies screamed.

"Sit still! Sit still!" yelled Gail. But no one paid any attention. The people were all standing up. They were yelling. The boat tipped over. Everyone was dumped into the water.

"Gail Borden," cried a woman, "my dress is ruined. You are the craziest man in town!"

One of the men was laughing. "Gail Borden has dozens of inventions, and he is the most wonderful one of them all!"

Good Citizen

"What did you do at the alderman's meeting tonight?" asked Penelope, holding the new baby Mary Jane.

"The usual," said Gail. "We set some more rules about businesses. We are trying to make Galveston a better place to live."

Penelope looked at her husband. She knew people thought he was odd, but she knew he was a good man. "I'm proud of you," she said, "especially the way you ran the gamblers out of Galveston."

Gail sat down at the table and stretched his legs. "We have to build a new jail," he said. "Today a prisoner dug through the soft walls of the old one."

Then he jumped up and grabbed a piece of chalk in each hand. At the blackboard on the wall he began to draw a picture of the island. "The worst

31

news is that Santa Anna may be planning to invade Galveston. I plan to build a fort here on the east end of the island. We'll be safe then."

Penelope served Gail's plate. "Pastor Burleson came by today. He wants to start a college. They want you to be a trustee."

Gail's face grew thoughtful. "I'm not sure I would be good at that," he said. "But we need a college. I'll do it!"

The trustees named the school Baylor University. It was located in a town named Independence.

Yellow Fever

Gail Borden paced up and down the room. "There must be a way," he said. "There must be a way."

Penelope sat by little Stephen Austin's bed. Gail looked down at his son. "He's just five years old. We can't let him die of yellow fever," said the weary father.

All their hope did no good. Little Stephen died.

Then six months later Penelope became ill with yellow fever. Gail could not save her either.

At the cemetery he stood beside her grave with his five children. Baby John Gail was not even a year old.

Sadness filled Gail's days. He could not sleep. Day and night he tried to think of a way to get rid of yellow fever.

The weather grew colder, and the yellow fever went away. "That's it!" said Gail. "We'll put everyone in a big building and make it cold." He did not know that the cold weather killed the mosquitoes which carried the yellow fever.

Gail started carpenters to work immediately. "People will stay inside here," he said. "They won't get sick from yellow fever."

But nobody came to live inside the big, cold building.

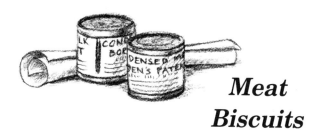

Meat Biscuits

Gail was lonely without Penelope. Before very long he married Augusta Stearns. For a wedding present, he made Augusta a table that turned in the middle so that you could get what you wanted without asking someone to pass the food.

The new Mrs. Borden didn't care for her husband's experiments. He was always trying to make some new food that nobody would eat.

Gail spent more and more time tinkering in his workshop and tending his fig trees. He kept account of his shorthorn cattle, Merino sheep, and potato crop.

One idea filled his mind now. He wanted to find a way to preserve meat so that travelers on long journeys would not get sick from eating rotten meat.

In his garage were steaming vats full of dark

liquid. Gail dipped out some and put the spoon to his mouth. "Hmmm, this needs to boil a little longer," he said, putting the spoon down.

"Don't forget," he told his two German helpers. "Put two pounds of this extract with three pounds of flour. This meat biscuit will save lives. You can bake it, put it in soup, and you can fry it. Nobody needs to go hungry again." His eyes danced with the thought of it.

He picked up a small, dark biscuit and put it in his mouth. Then he shook his head. "Too much flour in this." He opened the oven where meat was drying. "Grind up more dried meat in the next batch."

"Mr. Borden, you own more property than any-one else in Galveston. Why do you want to make these biscuits?" asked his helper.

Gail Borden nervously paced among the vats. "I just know that people like explorers need food that won't spoil. The army can use this meat biscuit. I'm going to sell it to them. Our new plant will be ready next week. We just have to get the right amounts of beef and flour."

That night Gail read an interesting article in the Galveston paper. The news told about a great ex-hibition to be held in Europe. "That's it!" said Gail. "I'm going to exhibit my meat biscuit in London."

Gail Borden was fifty years old when he sailed across the Atlantic. At the fair there were inven-tions from all over the world. His meat biscuit was exhibited along with the Colt revolver, the Mc-

Cormick reaper, and the Cornelius lamp. The meat biscuit won a medal.

Scientists in America said that the meat biscuit was one of the most valuable inventions that had ever been discovered. Gail spent a fortune making more and more meat biscuits.

The only problem was that people wouldn't buy it. The biscuit didn't look good, and it didn't taste good.

The army tried the meat biscuit, but they would not buy it either. They said they wanted only fresh meat and bread for the soldiers.

"What are we to do with all these?" asked one of the helpers, looking at the stacks and stacks of meat biscuits.

Finally, Gail hauled them out to the big building that was supposed to keep people from getting yellow fever. Nobody ever came to buy them.

Gail Borden lost nearly all his money — but not his imagination. "I never drop an idea except for a better one," he said.

He was already at work on a better idea.

Condense It

"It's a waste of time to sleep more than six hours a night," said Gail. "I've condensed my sleep and my eating. Everything should be condensed."

"Yeah," laughed Henry Lee. "Papa even told the preacher to condense his sermon because it was too long!"

Gail Borden kept working with his experiments. He was still haunted by the memory of the cries of the little children on the ship when he came home from Europe. They were sick because there was no milk to drink.

"Milk is the perfect food. I plan to condense it," he said.

Condensing milk would make it thicker, and it would last longer than regular milk.

Gail Borden went to New York, where there were good dairies. He would take fresh milk and try

Each failure made him try harder.

to condense it. Then the children of families going west would have good milk to drink.

He worked day and night. First he tried one thing, then he tried another. He couldn't find the right process to condense the milk. Each failure made him try harder.

While visiting a Shaker farm, Gail saw the way they heated milk in a vacuum pan that took all the air out. He used the pan. It worked!

Next he tried to get a patent on his condensed milk. For two years he kept going back and forth between New York and Washington. The man at the patent office got impatient. "You've brought me tons of paper about your product. The answer is still no!"

Gail did not give up. He kept going back. Finally, in 1856, he received United States patent number 15,553 for condensing milk in a vacuum pan at low heat.

The $350 Bride

When Gail was fifty-nine years old, he asked Mrs. Emeline Eunice Church to marry him.

On the day of their wedding, he sat down at a table. With a rare chuckle he looked up at her. "Brides are getting more expensive," he said. "When I married Penelope I only had to declare that I had $200. Now," he said, handing Emeline the piece of paper he had just signed, "this paper says that I will give you $350 a year as long as we are married."

Emeline may not have known that Gail borrowed $1,500 from his father that day. He had more ideas than money.

Emeline's sons, Alfred and Samuel, were nearly grown. They liked the honest, hardworking man who was their new stepfather. He might be eccentric, but he was kind.

Gail struggled to get his milk company started. He built a factory in Connecticut. He made lots of condensed milk, but nobody seemed interested. The factory had to close.

Then Gail tried again. He was sure people would buy his milk if they knew about it. He went from door to door in New York City selling the milk.

It was a discouraging time. The bank did not want to give Gail any more money. "I have failed," he said. "But I must not give up."

Friend and Partner

One day Gail was riding the train to New York. He turned to the stranger beside him. "I am Gail Borden," he said.

The younger man put out his hand. "My name is Jeremiah Milbank," he said. "I'm a grocer."

"Oh," said Borden, his dark eyes dancing as he started talking about his favorite subject. "Maybe you'd be interested in my patent. I have a way of making milk stay fresh."

Jeremiah Milbank listened as Gail talked. He liked the tall, intense man.

Gail explained, "I need a factory and more equipment to condense the milk. I am working on condensing fruit juice, too. I have even condensed coffee."

Jeremiah Milbank had a lot of money. He

watched Gail as he talked. He liked the honest face and the enthusiasm he saw. "I believe you, Borden," he said. "I like your ideas. I'll help you build your company."

That was the start of a long and happy partnership. Now there was money to manufacture the product and ways to advertise it. They built a factory in Wassaic, New York.

When the Civil War started, Gail's family was as divided as the country. John Gail was in the Union army. Henry Lee fought for the Confederacy. Gail remained in the North during the war. He believed along with Sam Houston that the Union should not be divided.

Oddly, the war which Gail hated became the reason for his company's success. The Union army ordered so much of his condensed milk that the Borden factory could not keep up with the requests.

The Milkcan

The Borden Milk Company was now a big success. Farmers wanted to sell their milk to the Borden Company, but they found that Gail set strict rules for cleanliness they had to follow. He personally went out to check the dairies. If a farmer broke the rules, no milk would ever be bought from that dairy again.

His son, John Gail, was working at the company, and so was his stepson, Alfred Church. For the first time in his life, Gail began to slow down. He was rich. He could do anything he wanted.

The Bordens had a large house in New York, but, as he grew older, the winters bothered Gail. Every year he went to Texas to escape the cold.

He bought land about seventy miles west of Houston and built a house for himself. His brother, John P. Borden, lived nearby. The town was called Borden.

Even though he was rich, Gail never lost interest in people or the community where he lived. In the town that had his name, Gail Borden built a freeman's school and organized a day school and a Sunday school for local children. He helped build five churches. He paid the salaries of two missionaries and gave money to students and poorly paid ministers and teachers.

Back in New York he did something that was unusual even for him.

One day a wagon with two men drove into Woodlawn Cemetery. The driver stopped at the gate and asked the caretaker, "Where is Gail Borden's grave?"

"Gail Borden is not dead," said the startled caretaker.

"I know it," said the driver. "I'm just supposed to put this up at the place where his grave will be."

The caretaker led the men to the plot. He watched as they uncrated their load. He just shook his head. "I've never seen anything like that before." He was staring at a huge granite milkcan.

The driver shrugged. "Borden's got enough money to do anything he wants. He made his money with milk. I guess he can have a milkcan to mark his grave."

But in 1874 the milkcan was taken away. Gail Borden had died in Texas on January 11. A special train took his body back to New York.

On Gail Borden's grave they placed a simple stone. It said,

I tried and failed.
I tried again and again, and succeeded.

46

Glossary

alderman — a member of a town council or other group that makes laws for the town.

condense — 1) to shorten in length; 2) to make milk thicker, with sugar added, in a process of evaporation.

customs house — a government office, often at seaports, which taxes goods brought into the country.

eccentric — having an odd or different behavior from the usual.

freeman — a word used to describe Blacks who had been freed from slavery.

militia — a group of persons, often citizens instead of soldiers, who are prepared to defend a community.

patent — a right given by the government to an inventor so that no one else may copy his invention for a certain amount of time.

retreat — to leave the scene of a fight by force of the enemy.

Shaker — a person belonging to a religious group of the eighteenth century which believed in a very strict and simple way of life.

steamer — another name for a steamboat.

surveyor — a person who measures the land so that its exact boundaries and characteristics are known.

topographic map — a map showing details of the land's surface.

vacuum — a process which removes air or matter.

vats — very large containers used to hold liquids.

Bibliography

Comfort, Harold W. *Gail Borden and His Heritage Since 1857.* New York: The Newcomen Society in North America, 1953.

The Dictionary of American Biography, Vol. I. (1957), "Borden, Gail."

The Handbook of Texas, Vol. I. (1952), "Borden, Gail, Jr.," by Joe B. Frantz.

Frantz, Joe B. *Gail Borden: Dairyman to a Nation.* Norman, Oklahoma: The University of Oklahoma Press, 1951. (out of print)

Gaines, John. "162nd Birthday Nears For Gail Borden, Isle Pioneer," *Galveston News,* November 4, 1962.

Shuffler, R. Henderson. "Gail Borden's Big Blunder," *Texas Magazine* of the *Houston Post,* February 27, 1966.

Werlin, Rosella H. "As Versatile as Da Vinci," the *Houston Chronicle Magazine,* June 1, 1947.

The Rosenberg Library, Galveston, Texas. Map of city and miscellaneous files, including one on Gail Borden.